THE

EXPERIMENT

Charlie—
Thanks for being
such a Ban!
YOU ROCK

9/25/14

FOR MORE INFORMATION
ABOUT MICHAEL VISIT
WWW.EXECUTIVEJOY.COM

The Experiment

Discover a Revolutionary Way to Manage Stress and Achieve Work-Life Balance

A business fable by
R. Michael Anderson, M.B.A., M.A.

Executive Joy! Publishing
San Diego, CA

R. Michael Anderson
Executive Joy! Publishing
2845 3rd Avenue, Unit 1B
San Diego, CA 92103, USA
www.executivejoy.com
www.experimenttoday.com
experiment@executivejoy.com

Ordering Information:
Quantity sales. Special discounts are available on quantity purchases by corporations, associations, and others. For details, contact us at experiment@executivejoy.com.

The Experiment / R. Michael Anderson —1st ed.
ISBN 978-0-9906605-0-7

Contents

Acknowledgements

My family: especially the two women in Austin and my two little brothers / writing partners at home.

My mentors, coaches & major influences: Ron & Mary Hulnick, Steve Chandler, Brian Tracy, Greg Godek (great book coach!), Chris Nelson (great editor!), Shannon Bindler (great marketing coach!), Tracy Suttles, Ron Harrell, Blake Canedy, Scott Bertone.

My Tribes: LV8, USM, EO, & NSA.

Contributors

These wonderful, powerful people gave great input and have much to do with the book you have here;

Adryanna Apellz

Martin Grunburg

Rachel Furman

Ellen Friedman

Bonnie Jarvis

Amy Hruby

Christina Hutto

Rory Cohen

Krista Clive-Smith

Laura Dewey

Scott Bertone

Thank you, truly.

The Experiment

One of Those Days

IT STARTED OUT AS one of those days for Dennis.

He was rushing to get to the office because his day was packed with meetings and phone calls. There was no room for error. And when he went out to his car to drive to work, it wouldn't start.

"Great," Dennis muttered. "Why do these things happen at the absolute worst times? What a way to start the day."

Dennis owned and ran a company that made electronic parts for the automotive industry. He'd started the company in his garage fifteen years ago and now his company was one of the largest in its field. Dennis was proud of being a "self-made man." He had learned to overcome the odds with hard work and fierce determination.

But none of that would help get his car started that morning.

He immediately started walking to the train station a quarter mile away. The commuter train came every half hour and would drop him off a few blocks from his office. As he walked to the station, he called his assistant and barked into the phone, "Cindy, my car won't start!"

Cindy had been with him and the company from the beginning so she knew not to take his tone personally. "Do you have the number of a shop near my house? Tell them I left the keys under the back left tire."

"Don't worry. I'll get you at the train station and we'll get started on our way back to the office. You won't miss a beat."

"Hmmph," he grunted as he hung up. Then he let out a sigh as he reminded himself that Cindy had just taken care of everything for him for the millionth time.

Dennis had to rush in order to catch the train; it was pulling up as he arrived at the station and he boarded just before the doors closed.

The train ride to his office would take twenty minutes and he didn't want to stand the whole time. He saw an empty seat beside a pleasant-looking man who appeared to be around Dennis' age, and who was wearing a nice suit. That seemed as good a place as any to sit, so Dennis took the seat. He and the man gave each other a nod as he sat down.

Dennis shut his eyes for a few minutes to think.

He was recently separated from his wife, Laura, and his thoughts drifted back to the times when she would drive him to work if he had car trouble, or if something else came up. But at the moment she and their two children, Sadie and Jacob, were living with her parents on the other side of town.

He was startled by a tap on his shoulder. The man in the suit sitting next to him said, "Your briefcase fell open." The man bent down, scooped up Dennis's papers and put them back into the case. Dennis felt himself get tense; there was a part of him that didn't like taking help from anyone, much less a stranger.

At that moment the train pulled in to his stop. Dennis forced a smile, gave the man a fast "thank you" and quickly squeezed out of the train.

Everyone Needs a Cindy

HE JUMPED INTO THE car with Cindy, who greeted him with a warm smile and chimed, "Hey Dennis! Good morning!" She had his coffee waiting for him—and Dennis even smiled a little bit.

Cindy began briefing him on the day. "First thing's the management meeting. We'll make it back in time, though I told Janice about your car just in case we're late. Then Leslie's coming in at ten. How's she doing anyway?"

Dennis had known Leslie, his banker, since he had founded the company. They had become friends and saw each other socially, even going on vacation with their spouses and kids from time to time.

"Not sure. Been awhile since we talked. I'm so busy I haven't had time to do much of anything else but work," replied Dennis.

After a silent moment Cindy said, "Remember when we opened that first bank account? You got us a savings account instead of checking? And we couldn't write any checks?" Cindy smiled broadly. "What a way to meet Leslie. She's been saving us from day one."

"Yeah," Dennis drawled. "She still reminds me about that. I tell her it's because I figured we'd need a savings account to hold the billions we were gonna make."

Cindy giggled as she deftly navigated the chaotic morning traffic. "She never bought that, did she?"

"Nah, she's way too sharp for that." He stared out the window at the traffic and said, "Ah, the early days, Cindy. Stuff was so simple. Buy stuff, make stuff, sell stuff. All we talked about was how fun it was gonna be when we got big."

"I know. And now we've done it. We're much bigger than *I* ever thought we'd get." She smiled and glanced at him. "Umm, don't take that the wrong way, chief."

"No, no—I hear ya. When we started I thought we'd grow to be a handful of people. Now we've got fifty!" He looked at her. "And you know what, Cindy?"

"What?"

"It seemed a lot more fun back then." He sighed and returned his gaze to the traffic.

The Grind

BACK AT THE OFFICE they jumped right into the meeting room. But for whatever reason the management meeting still started ten minutes late and quickly devolved into a "what's-wrong-now" session.

Janice, the outspoken VP of Marketing, brought up the question on everybody's mind: "Dennis, what are you going to do with Bob?"

Bob was a very productive—and extremely difficult—employee. Although he brought in over half of their new product sales, he was very disruptive around the office. Dennis, in addition to being the company President, was currently filling the role of VP of Sales, so Bob was his headache.

Dennis tried to reply without sounding worried. "Bob? Why? What happened now?"

Janice said, "Two of my staff just told me that if he talks to them like idiots again they're going to quit."

Dennis sighed. He had no good answer for this.

Frank, the Chief Financial Officer, and often the voice of reason in these matters, said, "Janice, can you just keep him away from your team? He's abrasive, no doubt about it. But he also brings in a lot of revenue."

This discussion continued for forty-five more minutes. When the meeting ran out of time the matter was still undecided; they would have to continue the conversation the following week. They didn't even get a chance to review any of the new marketing numbers or the sales funnel.

Dennis and Cindy were the last two to leave the meeting. He turned to her and said with frustration, "I can't believe we spent a whole hour together and didn't get one thing accomplished." She gave him one of her patented compassionate looks.

As he was walking down the hall back to his office, Frank popped his head out his door and said, "Dennis, you know we have to go over the check run." This was the meeting in which they decided which of their vendors to pay that month. Dennis knew this was coming; he also knew it was best to get it over with, so he went into the CFO's office.

Frank said, "I'm sorry. I know you don't like these meetings."

Dennis nodded. "It's okay, Frank. Let's just plow through."

Cash flow had been an issue for the last two quarters, something that had never happened before. Although he liked Frank, Dennis had come to hate these particular meetings. They reminded him of how the company was starting to get up against the wall. He knew Frank was working magic to keep paying everyone without letting the world know they were short on cash.

They buckled down and went through the list of payables, strategizing who to pay and who to hold off with a variety of excuses.

Feeling drained at only ten in the morning, he headed into to his next meeting. This was with Leslie, his long-time banker and friend. While always happy to see her, Dennis knew he couldn't hide the numbers from her. He almost felt like he was selling Leslie a false future.

"Hello, Leslie, great to see you!" he said, perhaps too enthusiastically. They hugged and sat down in his office to get to work.

While reviewing the financials and projections, she suddenly looked him in the eye and asked, "Dennis, what's wrong?"

He feigned ignorance with a weak, "Nothing, why?" but she called him out. "Really. Talk to me—friend to friend. I can see it on your face. What's going on?" He found himself desperately wanting to talk, but the fact was he was also afraid to open up to someone who controlled his entire line of credit—which the company relied on in order to operate.

"It's nothing, Leslie. Well, I mean, it's just with Laura and the kids moving out and my car breaking down this morning..." He shrugged. "It sometimes feels like things are working against me." Then, catching himself before he slid further into his woes, he blurted out, "But I'm a fighter—nothing I can't handle!" He said this a little too loudly to be believed, and this in turn prompted a skeptical look from Leslie. Nonetheless, they went on with the business at hand.

When they had finished Dennis returned to his office, feeling exhausted, like he was fighting a fight with no end and no chance of winning. He sat at his desk for a few minutes, just feeling hopeless, until he had to jump on a conference call and plow through his back-to-back meetings for the rest of the day.

Does It Ever End?

CINDY USED THE RIDE to the train station to catch him up on other events of the day.

"Dennis, did I tell you about Bob?"

"Uh, no. what about Bob?" Dennis asked, feeling himself tense up.

"Don't worry. Nothing bad happened. He just asked me to tell you he needs next Monday off."

"Did he say why?"

"No. Just said he had something to do."

This was not good. It had never happened before; Bob always saved his vacation days for the holidays and boasted about where he was going. Normally if he had a personal appointment, he would just work around it. Was Bob interviewing with someone else?

Dennis jumped out of the car just as his cell phone started ringing. It was his wife, Laura.

"Dennis, your daughter's in trouble again. She's hitting other kids at school." Their daughter, Sadie, was eight years old, and she was having a tough time dealing with the separation. Every time Dennis heard about another problem with Sadie his heart dropped. Laura could really get to him when she called Sadie "his daughter" when the girl was behaving badly. Of course, when Sadie did something good, she was "Laura's little princess."

Laura went on. "I need to get out of town this weekend. You need to take care of the kids. I'm dropping them off at noon on Friday."

"Laura, I can't, dammit. I have a full schedule and a business dinner on Friday! Don't dump this on me. Why are you doing this?"

Laura simply said, "Well, cancel your appointments and be a dad for once."

Dennis almost blew his top. He held back to keep himself from yelling at her at the top of his lungs. Just then he saw that the train had already stopped at the station. He growled into the phone, "I'll call you later," and hung up.

Who Is This Guy?

DENNIS STEPPED INTO the train, his mind racing, trying to figure everything out. He saw an open seat and without thinking threw himself into it—so hard in fact, that he felt himself smash into the passenger next to him; this caused the man to drop his tablet computer.

Great, thought Dennis, *I can't even take a train ride without something messing up.*

As the man picked up his tablet, Dennis recognized the suit and noticed it was the same guy whom he had sat next to on the ride to work that morning.

Dennis said, "Man, I'm sorry. Did I break it? I'll pay for a new one."

The man turned the device over, scanning for damage, then ran his fingers across the screen. He said, "It appears everything's fine." He smiled and looked Dennis directly in the eyes. His gaze was soft and warm. "Bad day?"

It was the first moment that day that Dennis was with someone who wasn't related to all the stresses surrounding him. He felt the need to let it all out. He slumped down, his shoulders drooped, and he said, "My work sucks, my wife hates me, my kids are having major problems... It's like life is beating me down."

The man looked at him with empathy, as if he were giving Dennis permission to open the floodgates, and this helped Dennis continue: "I'm so tired. I'm not even sure where I'm going. I'm trying so hard, and for once in my life it's not enough. I'm actually afraid I might lose it all. I don't know if I could handle that."

Dennis abruptly stopped speaking when he remembered that he didn't even know the person sitting next to him. The man continued to look straight at him, listening intently, waiting for him to continue. Dennis glanced around nervously; no one else was listening.

The man obviously sensed why Dennis had stopped. He smiled and said, "It's okay. Sometimes we just need to get it out. I'm Robert, by the way."

"Aaahh, thanks Robert. I'm Dennis. You must think I'm nuts."

Robert let out a small laugh and said, "If you're nuts, we're all nuts. We all go through ups and downs in our lives. You're just in a down. It'll turn around. It always does. The question is, what are you doing to solve it?"

"What do you mean?"

"Right now I hear you're going through a tough time. And I can tell that you care—you care about your company, you care about your family. When everything hits us all at once, we can go into 'firefighting' mode to just get through the day. How'd I do?"

"Yeah, that's it. It's like I can barely keep up. I'm just trying to stay far enough ahead to fight the next day."

Robert asked, "Can I suggest one thing for you to do tonight?"

Dennis replied, a little tentatively, "Uhmmm... I guess so." After all, who was this random guy on the train to offer him advice?

Then again, he thought, *I could use some.*

"Take each problem one by one and figure out how you want it resolved. You most likely haven't even thought about that since you've been so focused on survival. Ask yourself, what's your ideal outcome? That's the first step towards solving the problem itself, rather than just dealing with the symptoms."

Just then Dennis realized they were one stop past where he had to get off. It was still close enough to walk, so he grabbed his things, quickly shook Robert's hand and said, "Thanks Robert. Sorry for unloading on you. We don't even know each other. This isn't really like me."

"That's fine Dennis. I completely understand. This is what I do, anyway."

Dennis nodded, trying to take it all in as the bell dinged for the next stop. The doors opened and a rush of people pushed Dennis right out of the train.

Reflection

THE THIRTY-MINUTE WALK HOME worked out well for Dennis. It was refreshing and allowed him time to think, to ask, as Robert had suggested, how he wanted to resolve the problematic issues in his life.

Bob, the salesperson, was easy. Dennis wanted him to produce as a salesman and be a good team player. He didn't even have to be the number one cheerleader in the company. He just needed to quit pissing people off.

What did he want for his company? He wasn't really sure. At one point it had been fun—really fun. Now it wasn't. He had to psyche himself up every morning to even go into work. Even though he had been adapting to run a larger organization, he wasn't enjoying it.

His mind drifted to his family: Laura, Sadie and Jacob. They were who he lived for. He worked hard at his company to build a good living for them, even though the last few years he hadn't spent much time with them. When he thought of them now, a big, black cloud of negativity enveloped him. His relationship with Laura seemed so complicated; it felt like they weren't even on the same page anymore. Were things even salvageable?

This line of thinking got him even more depressed. How could he solve his issues if he didn't even know what he wanted?

And what did Robert mean when he said, "This is what I do?"

When he got home he heated up some food and sat down to eat in front of the television, along with a vodka and soda. He had poured in so much vodka that he almost gagged with his first swallow. He forced it down quickly so he could get to the second one.

A few more vodka sodas and a large dose of reality television deadened the evening and he fell asleep on the couch.

The Next Day

HE WOKE UP IN bed. At some point during the night he must have gotten up and gone to his bedroom. He felt groggy and had a dry mouth and a headache. Lying there, he thought about all the reasons he shouldn't get up. There were a lot of them, and right then they all sounded like they justified a day off.

With a seemingly herculean effort, Dennis pulled himself up and dragged himself into the shower. He was happy to be a little hungover as it dulled the thought of what awaited him that day. Caffeine gave him the added pickup he needed to jumpstart himself.

As he walked to catch his train he thought of the guy he had met yesterday. *Robert*—was that his name? The guy must have thought he was crazy. He would apologize if he saw him again.

Since the train from the suburbs into the city only ran every hour, it wasn't that surprising that he got his chance to see Robert sooner rather than later.

"Hey Robert," Dennis said as he sat down next to him, pausing to think about how to launch into an apology without looking even crazier.

"Good morning, Dennis," Robert said, and then beat Dennis to the punch: "You know, I was thinking of our conversation yesterday, and I just wanted to say thanks for being so vulnerable. I really feel honored anytime anyone opens up to me. That was really courageous on your part."

Dennis had certainly not been expecting this. He said, "Uh... sure. You're welcome." He remembered the question that had occurred to him as he was walking home the day before and added, "Yesterday as I was getting off the train you said, 'This is what I do.' What did you mean by that?"

Robert said, "I teach people. Mostly business people. I teach them to solve their problems."

"I don't understand. Are you a shrink?"

"Sort of, but not really," Robert said. "I focus on solving real-word issues rather than reliving old memories. Sometimes it can be helpful to do 'archeology'—that's what I call digging up the past, like they do in counseling. But usually I work on where people are *today*, and on moving them forward from there."

Dennis must have had a confused look on his face, because Robert continued explaining himself. "For example, you brought up several personal issues with me yesterday. Yet, here I am, a total stranger. My guess is that you don't have anyone else to talk to about these things. That is, anyone without their own agenda.

"When you're the boss you can't talk about heavy issues with your employees or coworkers. Your staff looks to you for leadership and it would get confusing.

"When you're married, even when it's going well, your spouse or partner may not want to know absolutely everything that's going on with you. Even if they do, they may not get the big picture. It can be difficult for them to understand what you go through every day, and they may not have the same tolerance for risk that you do. So talking about heavy decisions can stress *them* out.

"Friends can provide some help, but it's not always ideal to put your buddies in a situation where they have to tell you the difficult, crucial things you need to hear.

"That's where I come in. I provide people a force that is one-hundred percent devoted to solving their problems, and in their best interests. My sole agenda is their success."

Dennis said, "So you're a coach?"

"Yes," Robert replied. "Though I'm careful with that word. There are all sorts of coaches. And the truth of the matter is that anyone can call themselves a coach. Some call me a coach, some a consultant, some an advisor. Therapist, listener, teacher, pain-in-the-butt... I guess I'm a little of all of them."

Dennis smiled and was now curious. "So how do you become, well, whatever you are?"

"In my case it was through a lot of learning the hard way. I had a few businesses myself. At one point I found myself in much the same place you are, although my first business failed. And I can tell you that was the hardest thing I ever went through in my life."

"How did the second one do?"

"It was very successful, then I sold it."

"Did you do anything different the second time around?"

"Yes. I got a coach."

"Ha! Well played," said Dennis. "So then, Master, now that you know my problems, what do I do?"

Robert chuckled. "Well first of all, I don't know all the answers. I can offer you some strategies that have worked for others, and you can experiment with them. And I also know a process you can follow and the kinds of questions to ask so that *you* can figure out what to do."

"You mean you're going to go all Yoda on me?"

Robert smiled. "You could say that, yes. Though I'm no good with a lightsaber. Much better with a smartphone."

"Okay. So ask me the questions so I can get some answers."

"Sure. Between now and the next stop we'll have everything figured out."

"Seriously. I'm starting to understand. I need help. Really. So tell me, how does it actually work?"

"It's difficult to explain the coaching process; it's something that should be experienced. We can schedule a session together. It will take at least an hour or two, and we'll dig into the issues *beneath* the issues. At the end you'll have an idea of what this type of coaching can bring you. And I can tell you this: every person I've ever had a session with has gotten something out of it. Every one."

Dennis and Robert set a time late the next afternoon to meet.

Cold Feet

THE NEXT DAY, a few hours before his appointment with Robert, Dennis was hit with the normal barrage of stuff at work. He was considering moving the appointment when Cindy stopped in to have him sign some papers.

She asked, "What's this appointment with this 'Robert' person coming up?"

"Oh. He's some guy I just met on the train."

Cindy gave him a questioning look. It wasn't like Dennis to meet people on trains, much less then set up meetings with them.

Dennis sensed what she was thinking and said, "He's a coach."

"What sport?" she asked, still confused.

"No sport. He's like a business and personal coach."

"What does he help with?"

"I'm not sure. Maybe figuring out what I'm doing and how to do it better, or differently, I guess." Dennis glanced at all the papers on his desk and said, "But, you know, I'm getting busy. I'm gonna cancel. In fact, can you call—"

"No way," Cindy said, cutting him off.

While this was not out of the norm for Cindy—she felt comfortable speaking her mind and was almost always on the money—it still caught him off guard.

Cindy said, "If there's any chance this guy can help you, go meet with him. Dennis, you're such a Type A personality it's going to kill you. You put so much on your plate, both here and at home. It's time you get some support for yourself."

While this was meant to be supportive, it nonetheless made Dennis feel slightly defensive. He said, "I don't know. I'm not sure it'll even help."

Cindy looked at him thoughtfully for a moment, then said, "Have one meeting with the guy. What the heck—call it an experiment."

Session 1

Fundamentals & Ground Rules

THE FIRST THING Robert did when they met was give Dennis the ground rules.

"Everything we say together is held in the utmost confidence. I encourage you to go as deep as you can in working through your issues with me. The more you're open, the more you go for it, the more you'll get out of this. It's really up to you. What do you say?"

Dennis hesitated. After a moment's thought he shrugged his shoulders and said, "Okay, what the heck." Robert gave him a look that he must have perfected over the years, because it clearly said, *Are you sure?* In response, Dennis sat up straight and declared with enthusiasm, "Yes. Let's do this—I'm in one-hundred percent!"

Robert smiled. "Great. Let me tell you about a simple system to support you through this. I'm a long-time basketball player." Dennis had noticed Robert was on the tall, lanky side. "Now when you shoot a basketball, what shape does the basketball travel in?"

Dennis answered, "Well, it travels in an arc."

"Exactly," Robert said. "An arc. A-R-C. Three letters, three steps, very easy to remember. And A-R-C is what we apply to the situations we want to address. 'A' is for Awareness, 'R' is for Response, and 'C' is for Compassion."

"Sounds simple enough, 'ARC.'"

"Simple yet complex."

Dennis raised one eyebrow and smiled.

Robert laughed and asked, "Too much Yoda?"

"It's okay. I'm with you."

A is for Awareness

"LET'S START WITH the 'A' for Awareness. What this re-fers to is that we need to be aware of what is going on both externally in the outside world and, more importantly, inter-nally within us. Sometimes awareness hits us like a ton of bricks. For example, can you feel it when you're getting angry or anxious?"

"Yes, sometimes," Dennis answered. "Other times I don't feel it until I'm already there."

"You're right. Sometimes we don't have the awareness until later, or until we check in with ourselves to connect to it.

"What do you mean by 'check in'?"

"Good question. I mean *stop*. Stop whatever you're doing, stop what you're thinking, and concentrate on what's pre-sent. It's easier than it sounds. And it normally only takes a moment. Got it?"

Dennis nodded. "I think so."

> **Checking in is as simple as slowing way down and paying attention to where we are, mentally and emotionally. The more clear we are with what's going on inside us, the more powerful the next step will be.**

R is for Response

"GOOD. SO ONCE WE have Awareness, we come to Response. To understand what we mean by Response, let's start with talking about control."

Dennis chuckled. "I'm good at control! Ask my wife and kids."

Robert grinned. "Yeah. And you're probably the first business owner ever to say *that*." They both laughed, and Robert continued, "But really. Let's dig into this. What can you actually control?"

Dennis said, "A lot."

"Can you control whether or not you hit your profit targets this year?"

"Well... I want to say 'yes,' even though I know that sometimes we don't. But I do have a lot to do with it."

Robert nodded. "Absolutely. At the very least you can certainly influence it. You can control what you do and how you do it. But at the end of the day, something catastrophic, something completely out of your control may happen. The industry might take a turn downwards. Or a big customer might go out of business. All of that kind of thing is out of your control. So ask yourself again, what do you truly have control over, and what don't you?"

"I have control over my people."

"Do you really?"

This made Dennis think. "Well, yeah, sort of..."

"What do you mean, 'sort of'?"

"I can motivate them, give them clear goals, hire and fire them."

"Well look at your answer. You're talking about what *you* can do in relation to them. But can you *directly* control them?"

"No, I guess not."

"So what *can* you control?"

"I guess I can control what I do."

"Exactly. We can control ourselves. What *can't* you control?"

"Them?"

"That's right. We can control ourselves. That's it. Everything else we can't control. We can influence people and circumstances through what we do, but we can't directly control them. Stress comes from trying to control things we can't control."

Dennis thought about this for a minute. He scanned through the things he was stressed about: cash flow, his wife and kids, Bob... Sure enough, his stress came from things he couldn't directly control.

All he could muster to say as this sunk in was: "Wow."

> We can only control ourselves. We can *influence* people and circumstances through what we do, but we can't directly control them. *Stress* comes from trying to control things that are out of our control.

Dennis' Notes—Stress and Control

What I CAN control	What I CAN'T control
Me, Myself and I	Everyone and Anything else

Awareness: Where in my life am I experiencing stress? What am I trying to control?

Response: I'm going to STOP attempting to control something I can't. Instead, what CAN I control in the situation?

Download Dennis' notes at **www.experimenttoday.com/exercises

Shift into Ownership

ROBERT GAVE HIM a moment before continuing, "There are two parts to this equation: letting go of things you can't control and taking ownership of things you can. There is an incredible amount of stuff that we *can* control, though we may not realize it. And when we don't take ownership of what we control we are showing up as the victim. It can be easier to play the victim. But when we move from victim to owner, we can do incredible things.

"This is the Owner/Victim choice. Instead of playing a victim, you can choose to show up as an owner. Victims don't choose a response, they just complain and feel bad for themselves. Owners remember that their response is a choice."

> Victims don't choose a response, they just complain and feel bad for themselves. Owners remember that they have dominion over their state of being through their choices and actions.

Dennis said, "I'm not sure this is totally sinking in."

"Okay, let me give you an example. Let's say at work you lose a big customer. What's the first thing that goes through your mind?"

"Well... I get angry, of course. I'm upset."

"Yes, exactly. It's okay, even natural, to feel those feelings. We're human. That upset is what I call a 'reaction.' The reaction is what we feel normally and naturally. It's important to honor that, to be okay with whatever the reaction is. Now remember ARC—Awareness, Response, Compassion - we've reacted, then we want to be *aware* of where we are. Once we allow ourselves the reaction and the awareness kicks in, then we can start choosing our responses. Reaction is the automatic feeling that comes up. Response is the action or state of mind we then choose. So in this example, what are some helpful responses you could choose when you've lost a customer?"

Dennis thought for a minute and said, "Well there are a few things. One might be to try to get the customer back. If I can't do that, I might go out and find more business to replace them. I'd also want to find out why we lost them so it doesn't happen again."

"Great. Now what if we made a company rule for what to do every time we lose a customer. First we call and try to get them back. If that doesn't work, we make it a rallying call for our sales team to go out and find double the revenue to replace the old customer on top of their normal quota. Then we have an all-company meeting to find out why we lost them, and vow never to lose a customer like that again. What effect would that approach have on a company?"

Dennis could see the answer immediately. "It would make us strong. I think I get what you're saying. We're taking something that would normally would be a negative and making it a positive."

"Yes, Dennis. Exactly. Because at the end of the day losing a customer happens. That's business. When that happens it's normal to get a little upset. Once you have the Awareness, choose your Response. High-achievers use everything they can for their advantage. Make it work for you. *Own it.* That's the second part of ARC."

Dennis' Notes—Owner / Victim

We can often see how we are showing up as an owner or a victim by looking at the language we are using to describe something in our life.

Common clues:

Victim	Owner
I don't know how / I can't	I'll figure it out
I'll be happy if/when	I choose to be happy
I might commit	I am committing
I don't have time	I am making time
Life happens **to** me	Life happens **for** me

Additional words/phrases which can help identify owner or victim;

Victim	Owner
Negative	Positive
Blaming	Solutions/Supportive
Entitled	Accountable
Defensive	Proactive

Helpless	Helpful
Tardy/Late	Punctual/Early
"They"	"We/I"
"I Should…"	"I Will…"
"But…"	"And…"
"It's not fair"	"It doesn't matter"
"I Can't…"	"I Can…"
"I Don't Know"	"I'll Find Out"

Awareness: Where in life am I showing up as a Victim?

Response: How can I show up as an Owner?

Download Dennis' notes at **www.experimenttoday.com/exercises

C is for Compassion

DENNIS NODDED enthusiastically. "Hey, I think I'm getting it! OK, Yoda, you're right. It's simple—but it might take some getting used to in real life. How about the 'C'? Did you say it stands for 'compassion'?"

"Yes. So let me ask you, do you have the same little voice in the back of your head that I have? The one that keeps chattering? Mine used to be great at telling me all the things I didn't do perfectly, and how things were never going to work out in my favor."

"Oh, yeah. I sure do."

"When we have some kind of realization or learn something new, we often get angry at ourselves for 'shoulda' knowing it already, or for not being perfect. Now instead of doing that, we learn to have compassion for ourselves."

This made Dennis pause. "Yeah... That little voice often points those things out to me."

"It's okay —so did mine. And yours still will, for a while at least. But that doesn't mean you have to *listen* to it. Again, we want to take ownership and choose our responses here as well. When we hear the voice and it isn't supportive, we simply change it."

"It's that easy?"

"Yes, it really is. When you find you're being hard on yourself, find a way to instead *prize* yourself—by 'prizing' I mean giving yourself credit, lifting yourself up, picking out some *positive* things that are going on. Train the voice inside you to start pointing out the good things you do instead of the problems and failures."

Dennis took this in. "That sounds good in theory. But I'm so far away from that right now that it seems impossible."

> **Self-compassion is vital to true inner joy and happiness. When we catch ourselves in negative self-talk, we can move right into positive self-talk and start changing our inner dialogue. Let's 'prize' ourselves: pat ourselves on the back for being aware and changing course, and remind ourselves of all the great things we do.**

What's it Like to Be YOU

"THAT'S ALRIGHT. That's something we'll work on. For today, the next thing I would like is for you to tell me this: What's it like to be Dennis?"

The question startled him. "What do you mean, 'What's it like to be Dennis?'"

"Just what I said: what's it like inside there?" He pointed at Dennis' chest. "How do you feel most of the time? How do you see the world?"

Dennis got very quiet—then suddenly very sad. His shoulders drooped and he thought about all the things weighing on him. Work, family, himself. He noticed Robert was looking at him, and knew Robert could sense what he was feeling. What made it okay was the compassion he felt from Robert. He knew he wasn't going to be judged, just accepted. When Dennis realized this, he was comforted; he knew this was a safe time and place.

He started speaking slowly, then the words began tumbling out. "It's... it's *hard*. Right now, especially. I don't even trust myself. I hate my life. I can't believe I'm saying that. But I *do* hate it. It's hard for me to admit. It's like I'm failing. And I can't see a way out. I'm tired. I feel boxed in. It's like someone, something is out to get me."

Robert simply maintained his soft, warm gaze.

Dennis continued, "I just keep plowing ahead. I don't even know where I'm going. I just live day-to-day. I have these huge boulders in my life and when I think of how big they are, I get panicked. I keep thinking that if I can just make it to the next day, maybe something will happen. I'm constantly living in fear. Fear that someday everything will get taken away. And it's weird, but even when something goes my way, I don't trust it. It's almost like something really bad must be coming if something good just happened. You know, when's the other shoe gonna drop?"

Dennis glanced down at the floor, absorbed in his own thoughts. He was starting to have that familiar feeling he got when he opened up to someone. In spite of Robert's patient and kind demeanor, Dennis was wondering how stupid he looked in front of this guy he had really just met.

After some time, Robert spoke. "It's okay Dennis. I hear you. This is all part of your process. It's okay to feel like that. In fact, this is really great. You're showing courage by opening up, by being honest with me and, more importantly, with yourself. The first step is acknowledging where you're at. So let me ask, how are you feeling right now?"

Dennis sighed and almost thought he was going to cry. His first inclination was to close down. Then he remembered his intention to "go for it" in this session.

He heard a slight tremor in his voice as he said, "I feel like life is out of control. I'm angry. Angry at everyone. Angry at myself. I'm tired of feeling this way. And scared. To be really honest with you, I'm scared."

Again Robert gave Dennis some time—something he seemed to be very good at doing—and with the warmest touch Dennis had ever heard, Robert said, "Thank you."

Dennis said in surprise, "For what?"

"For being willing to be honest and get vulnerable. When you get to that point, you're also ready to accept and then start moving on from there."

"I'm sure ready to move on."

The Difference between Joy and Happiness

"LET'S DO THAT, then. First we'll start with joy. Do you know the difference between joy and happiness?"

"No."

"Not many people do. Both are great, and at times I use the words interchangeably. But there's an important difference. Happiness comes from external forces. Joy is *internally* stimulated. "

"I don't understand."

"Let me explain more. We become happy when something happens *to* us. Say we make a certain amount of money. We eat something delicious. And there's certainly nothing wrong with happiness, though it's fleeting. It can come and go quickly."

"I'm with you so far."

"Joy, on the other hand, comes from our internal feelings. Pride, love, compassion—all create joy. Here's an example: If someone gave you a million dollars right now, would you be happy?"

"You bet I would!"

"Of course. So would I. In fact, though, there've been studies done around happiness that show even in extreme situations—like winning the lottery or getting a big promotion—happiness lasts at most a few weeks."

"I can see that. What about joy?"

"Say you start a business and it creates a million dollars in income. The pride you have from building that company and creating something of value is *joy*. You may still be *happy* about the money, but the joy will last much longer."

Dennis thought for a moment. "That makes sense. On the other hand, I've created a business that at the moment I'm not so joyful about."

"You just need to put it back in perspective," said Robert. "I call this 'Reconnecting to your Joy.' Let's try it. Tell me about your company. Who started it?"

"Me."

"Did you buy it?"

"No. I literally started it out of my garage."

"OK. So how would you rate your success as a business owner on a scale of one to ten, with ten being the highest?"

"I don't know. A three or four."

"Got it. And is this an internet company or in some other fast growing industry?"

"Heck no. It's an automotive supply business. Our industry has been around for more than a hundred years. It's competitive and tough. Plus, car part suppliers have had a lot more downs than ups since we've started."

"And how big is your company?"

"We've got about fifty people, and eight million in revenue," said Dennis as he sat up straight.

"So let's round up and say you rate yourself a four."

"Okay."

"Then let's break this down. Did you know only four percent of companies generate over a million in revenue?"

"I knew the number was low. I didn't know it was *that* low."

"It is. I would guess that only one out of a hundred ever gets to over five million. And let's say only one in a hundred people ever starts a company. That's means you've done something that only .04% of the population has done. And you've done it in a mature industry in a down market."

Dennis felt a smile form on his face. "Wow. I never thought of it that way."

"Now let me ask you: how do you treat your employees?"

"We put a huge emphasis on our employees. In fact, that's what's kept us afloat over these last two years—the loyalty of our people."

"So there you go. You've created a place where fifty people can come to work, feed their families, and take pride in what they do. That's not a common thing, Dennis. In fact, it's very rare. I'll bet very few people could understand what you went through those first five to ten years when you were establishing your company."

Dennis felt a swelling sense of pride, and he smiled. "You're right. There were times where I thought we weren't going to make it. In fact, I would have bet against us a few times!"

Robert said, "Now taking all of that into account, how would you rate yourself as an owner and businessperson? Still a four?"

After a second of reflection, Dennis said, "I guess an eight or a nine."

"I would personally give you even closer to a ten. Now do you feel proud of your company and what you've built?"

"Yes I do."

"There you go. That's reconnecting with your joy."

> **Joy is always inside of us. It's an endless source of positive energy we can simply bring forward. It takes a conscious effort, but we can choose the response that reconnects us with our joy at any time.**

Experimenting with Experiments

"HMMM. I THINK I get that, thanks. But, you know, the problem is that when I start thinking like that I get worried I'll lose my 'edge.' Now that I think about it, it's like my drive comes from thinking I'm at a four or five, so I have to work harder to get to my goals."

"Let's look at that. Have you hit your goals before?"

"Yes."

"Did that make you happy?"

"Well, I celebrated for an instant. But I didn't want to get complacent. Actually, to be truthful I was a little angry at myself for taking so long to hit my goals. And then I set new ones—higher ones."

"So if I'm hearing you correctly you think that if you're happy you won't be driven."

"I guess so," Dennis said hesitantly. "Yeah. In a way I think that's true."

"Sounds like a tough way to go through life."

"I don't know any other way."

"Well that's why we're here today: to start learning new ways to go through life. Can you simply be open to the idea that you can be happy, joyful and content—all while being even *more* successful than you are right now?"

"Hmmm. Honestly, I'm hesitant."

Robert nodded. "That's understandable. We're talking about changing one of your core beliefs, and that can bring about some resistance. What normally happens is that people *do* want to change, but the thought of changing a core belief is too much. They either simply don't want to commit, or they say they'll commit—and maybe even think that they will—but aren't truly all in."

"Yup. You just nailed it. Those thoughts have been with me my whole life. I can't truthfully say I'm going to change right now."

"And you shouldn't. We want to ease into this process, to play with it. We want to try different things and see if they stick. If they don't, we'll try something else. No pressure."

"How do we do that?"

"We bring the changes in as an experiment."

"An experiment? Ha! That's the second time I'm hearing that idea today."

"Great. Then you may know that there are great advantages to trying new things as experiments. There is no success or failure in an experiment, unless you don't even give it a try. That's the nature of experiments."

> **There is no success or failure in an experiment. We win just by conducting it. To start an experiment, take a small, bite-sized piece of the task with a very short timeframe. The only objective is learning.**

Dennis nodded and said, "It sounds a lot less intimidating, too. It's like I can make changes at any time. I'm not committing to it forever. It's easy to jump in and try."

Robert said, "Exactly. For a period of time, we'll try out a new way. If that doesn't work, you can go back to the old way. Or we can try something else. We'll give it a set amount of time, a trial run if you will."

"Like, instead of trying to make a change for the rest of my life, I make the change for the next three days and see how it works?"

"You got it."

Dennis exhaled deeply. "Tons easier. I'm in for that. Let's experiment."

Dennis' Notes—Experiments

Remember, I succeed in experiments just by conducting them. Experiments are meant to test waters. I can modify them any time I choose. The reason I go through an experiment is to try one possible solution to an issue and learn from it.

Awareness: Where in my life am I experiencing procrastination, resistance, and/or fear? What do I want to change?

Response: How can I make that into an experiment? What will I change? For how long?

Compassion: I'm kind to myself as I go through the experiment. The goal is to learn, try new things, and see what works for me.

Download Dennis' notes at **www.experimenttoday.com/exercises

What about Bob?

"GREAT. SO THEN let's take a situation going on with you right now, something that's causing stress. What's the first one that comes to mind?"

Dennis answered right away. "That's an easy one. My top salesperson, Bob, has become a real problem around the office. We butt heads every time we get near each other. I don't even go into the sales room anymore when he's there. Other people have been complaining about him as well. It's a real issue in our company."

"Does he produce?"

"Yeah. He's been with us for five years, knows everyone in the industry, and brings in over half of our new product sales. But he's causing so much tension in the office that I'm planning on firing him."

Robert looked impressed. "Wow. Over half your sales. If you let him go, what would be the effect on your business?"

"Well on the one hand it'll create a better atmosphere around the office. On the other hand, down the road it may mean we have to lay people off." He sighed. "To be honest, I'm not even sure if we could survive that kind of hit. He just really pisses me off! All he does is brag about how great he is. Though it's his own fault. He—"

Robert raised his hand to stop Dennis. "Hold on. I'm not a referee. I'm here to help you move forward, not figure out who's to blame."

> **Solutions aren't about who's right or wrong. They're not about arguing about the past. They're about creating a great future.**

"OK. Understood."

"How have you handled it up until now?"

"When I see him acting like an ass, I let it go once or twice, then I try to put him in his place."

"How do you do that?"

"I'll pick out something I can pick on him for. Then I'll call him out in front of everyone. I figure I have to keep him humble while I show everyone I'm still in charge. Otherwise his ego will get even bigger."

"How's that tactic been working for you?"

Dennis sighed. "Not good. It usually ends up getting heated. Both of us get defensive and start yelling at the other one. Often in front of other employees."

"That doesn't sound good at all."

"It's not—and it's getting worse. It's come to a head. I need to do something soon. Like this week—or staff may start leaving. I've had several 'it's-Bob-or-me' conversations already."

"Let's try taking a different path."

"Yeah. But what?"

"Instead of making him wrong, why not make him right?"

"I don't get it."

"Hear me out. You've been focusing on what he's been doing wrong. What about supporting what he's been doing right? Ask him how you can treat him better?"

"I could never do that!" Dennis said loudly, tensing up.

"Why not?"

"Because he's wrong! He's so arrogant!"

"Well, it sounds to me like you really are the victim here."

Dennis crossed his arms and looked at Robert, surprised. "How am I acting like the victim?"

"Remember we talked about how we can either show up as an owner or a victim in any situation. Right now you're focused on what he did rather than what you're going to do. How can you make this situation work for you?"

> **If we're victims, life is happening *to* us. "Woe is me. My life stinks. Everyone is against me." But if we show up as owners we take control of the situation. Life happens *for* us. We look at what we can control and work with that.**

"Hmmm," Dennis mumbled skeptically. "So what do you suggest?"

"You can't control Bob. But you can control what you do and say to him. What about asking him how you can better support him?"

Dennis replied firmly, "There is no way I'm doing that."

Robert shrugged. "Okay, then, when will you start your layoffs?"

Dennis paused. "I get your point. Okay." He thought for a moment. "So what would showing up as an owner look like?"

Robert countered, "You tell me. What would it look like?"

After a minute of thought Dennis said, "I like taking people out of the office for conversations like this. I could ask him to lunch."

"Sounds like a good idea."

"And then," Dennis continued with a sigh, "I could fall on a sword."

Robert said, "Let's pause for a second. This isn't about falling on a sword. This is about you taking ownership and showing leadership. Stepping up. Being mature. If you don't mean the words you say, what do you think will happen?"

"He'll see right through me."

"Yes, he probably will. Good salespeople are especially good at that kind of thing."

"So tell me how this is about me being a leader."

"This isn't about giving up your power. It's about bringing power *to* your relationship with Bob. Positive power."

"So I'm going to acknowledge him and appreciate him—and ask what else I can do to support him?"

"Yes."

Dennis felt himself loosening up. "Hmmm... An experiment, right?"

"What do you have to lose?"

"Half my sales."

"Exactly. For now, try it and see what happens. You can always fire him later. But, really, let's save that for when we've run out of alternatives. Like you said, think of it as an experiment," said Robert, a sly grin playing on his lips.

Showing Up as a Leader

THE NEXT DAY Dennis approached his star salesperson a few minutes before noon.

"Bob, I looked at your calendar and saw you're free for lunch. Let me take you out to Sally's Diner. I know you like that place. We'll break bread together." Dennis did his best to sound upbeat. He knew that Bob would take an invitation to lunch as a sign he was getting bad news, maybe even that he was about to be let go.

Bob looked away and said, "Dennis... I... I don't think so. I've got a lot of work to do here. What's all this about anyway?"

"Bob, don't worry. It's not what you think. I just want your input on something. Really." Dennis felt uncomfortable with the whole process, but he was trying hard to be genuine and authentic. He even managed a real smile, which must have helped, because Bob agreed to go.

After a short car ride consisting largely of tension and small talk, they arrived at the diner, took a booth near the window, and ordered.

"Bob," Dennis said, looking into his rainmaker's eyes, "I simply want to tell you that you've been doing a great job. I just wanted to say thank you."

Bob shifted his gaze and looked at Dennis sideways. "And...?" Bob said.

"It's obvious we've had a strained relationship lately. As the boss, I take full ownership of that. I'm also taking responsibility for getting us back on track. The fact is, you're a great salesperson. What do you need from me? What can I do to make this a better place for you to work?"

Now that the message was out, Dennis felt relieved. He looked at Bob, who wasn't moving. After a minute, Dennis could swear he saw Bob twitch and hold back a tear. When the response came, it came like an avalanche.

"Dennis, *thank you*. Thank you so much. I've always really respected you. I bust my hump for this company. It means so much for me to hear that from you. I think all this bad blood started when—"

Dennis held up his hand. "Hold on, Bob. I'm sorry to interrupt. But we don't need to dig into the past. That doesn't matter. Let's just move forward from here." He chuckled to himself as he heard Robert's voice saying the same things in his mind. Then he thought, *This isn't so hard after all.*

Session 2

Remember - Compassion

THE NEXT TIME he met with Robert, Dennis entered his office and sat down quickly. He said with excitement, "Well, I did it! You won't believe what happened."

"I might," Robert replied with a grin.

Dennis filled Robert in on the lunch. Then he reflected, "Before we sat down, I was dreading telling him he was a great salesman and asking how I could support him. But once I did it, it felt good. And the look on his face... He couldn't believe what he was hearing! Then he talked for the whole rest of the lunch. I barely said a word. I just nodded and let him get it out. And it turns out he has some great ideas. Like, *really* great. He just figured no one was listening so he never bothered to share them. And to be honest, he was right: we wouldn't have listened."

Robert nodded and grinned.

Dennis continued, "It was amazing that a simple conversation like that could turn things around, especially so fast.

People came up to me later that afternoon and asked, 'What's up with Bob?' He was so happy and helpful they thought we must have split a bottle of wine over lunch! He even spent some time telling *Janice's* team how they were doing a great job. She was bowled over—and so was I. Can it be that simple?"

Robert smiled. "Yes, indeed. Yes it can."

Suddenly the smile dropped from Dennis' face. Robert looked at him questioningly, and in response Dennis said, "This is all great, but why didn't I do this sooner? Man! It's such a simple change. I'm such an idiot. All that wasted time! I almost fired him!"

Robert said, "Hold on there. Slow down. Remember the 'C' in the ARC system? Compassion?"

"Yes," Dennis said.

"What you're going through now is exactly why compassion is part of the system. Be easy on yourself."

Dennis leaned back and took in a deep breath. "Okay. I see. But it's hard. I have such high expectations for myself."

"I know, and that's very common. It's just not healthy. You won't move ahead if every time you learn something new you get down on yourself. Be aware of how you're treating yourself."

"So what do I do when I catch myself doing that?"

"Simply change the negative talk to positive talk. Awareness, response, compassion. It's a simple concept, though it takes some time to learn the new habit."

Dennis' Notes—Positive Self-Talk

Awareness: Where am I getting down on myself and engaging in negative self-talk?

Response: How can I look at the situation from a different, self-supporting angle?

Compassion: All people drop into self-criticism at times. It's called being human. But just because it's natural doesn't mean we have to stay there!

Download Dennis' notes at **www.experimenttoday.com/exercises

Habits & the Bush

"THAT'S A HABIT?"

"Yes. My Australian friend explains that creating these new habits is like walking through the bush, which is like an Australian forest. If you have a path going through the bush that you've been using your whole life, it's well-worn and easy to walk through. Now say you find a way through that's only half as long. What's the problem with going that way?"

"Well, it's probably overgrown, isn't it?"

"That's right. In fact, you have to cut your way through it the first time. But then each time you take the new faster, better path, it's easier. Over time, what happens to the old path?"

"It gets grown over."

"Correct. It just doesn't happen overnight. It takes some time to open up these new ways of thinking, to create these new habits and forget the old way of doing things. After a while, though, it becomes second nature."

"So every time I catch myself criticizing myself, I should make the adjustment?"

Robert nodded. "Yes. I call that changing from negative to positive self-talk. Or you can think of it as developing a new path."

"What if I forget and go back to the old way?"

"I'll give you a very easy way to keep these ideas in the forefront of your mind. Is there a place you can put a whiteboard in your house? Someplace where you'll always see it?"

"Sure. In my kitchen. I'm in there a few times every day."

"Okay. Go ahead and hang one up there. Then draw a column for each new habit you want to create, including the kinds of things we're talking about here. Let's use self-compassion as an example. Once a day, think of a time where you were compassionate with yourself and make a 'check' in the column. Since you'll be focusing on your self-compassion level every day, you'll learn to be aware of when you're criticizing yourself and when you're choosing a more healthy response. It's building that muscle, slowly and surely."

"Sounds easy."

Changing behavior is simply a matter of developing new habits. Any behavior we have can be changed by giving it attention and moving into the new, desired behavior.

Dennis' Notes—Habits

Awareness: What is a habit I want to change?

Response: I'm creating a checklist where I will track what I want to change.

Habit	Monday	Tuesday	Wednesday
Hug my kids	√	√	√
Prize myself	√	√	√

Compassion: It's not about judging where I am; rather it's about moving forward and blazing that new path through the bush!

Download Dennis' notes at *www.experimenttoday.com/exercises*

Why Wait for Happiness?

"NOW, BACK TO the situation with Bob. You were down on yourself about how you didn't take these steps up until now. How can you change your thinking around that?"

"Well... I learned a heck of a lot. This one episode made me a better boss and leader. It's opening up a whole new world."

"Yes," said Robert. "And I bet it took a lot of courage to take that step."

"Courage..." Dennis thought about this for a moment. "Yeah, I guess it did. I sure didn't want to do it, but I did anyway."

"That sounds like courage to me."

"I see that now." He smiled. "Hmmm. I *did* do some good work!"

Robert chuckled and said, "Now you're getting it! Should we move on to something else in your life that's not working as well as it could?"

"Okay," Dennis said. But as he started to consider all of the things on his mind he tensed up. "Well," he stammered. "There's... there's just so much." The feeling of hopelessness crept back into him.

Robert seemed to sense this sudden shift and he said gently, "Hey, it's okay. Slow down there. Let's take one thing at a time. We're not going to solve everything today, right this minute. If you have that many things on your mind, let's focus on *you*. Tell me about your work/life balance. For example, how well are you taking care of yourself?"

Dennis looked up at the ceiling and slowly shook his head. "Not well. Not well at all. I've been drinking too much. Eating garbage. Now I feel sluggish all day. I haven't been exercising and I've been working a ton of hours. And it seems there's always more to do on my desk. I keep telling myself that once we get back to profitability I'll get in shape and start letting myself be happy again."

Robert said simply, "Hmmm."

Dennis couldn't help but smile. "Alright Yoda. What do you mean, 'Hmmm'?"

"What you're saying, Dennis, is that you won't be happy or in shape unless you're making money."

"Well... Yeah, I guess that's what I'm saying."

"Why?"

"I don't know. I don't have the time. I need to get the company back on its feet."

"I hear you. So my next question is, do you really think that sacrificing yourself is the way to do that?"

"I... I don't know what you mean."

Robert cocked an eyebrow and said, "I hear you saying that being happy and in shape is dependent on your business doing well. But the technical term for that is 'B.S.' Your happiness is your choice. So is being fit. The thought that you will become happy when something else happens is a myth."

Dennis looked at him in surprise.

Robert continued, "Instead of thinking in terms of 'OR' (I can be happy OR wealthy), or 'IF/THEN' (IF I become wealthy, THEN I'll become happy), think of things in terms of 'AND.' I am happy AND working towards being wealthy. I am in shape AND doing well at work.

"I can tell you without a doubt that when you're joyful, connected and in shape, you'll show up as a better leader.

You'll have more energy and focus, and you'll get considerably more done in less time."

> *Waiting* for happiness is the same thing as saying we are going to live an *unhappy* life in the meantime. Happiness is always right in front of us. Quit waiting. Look to change "OR's" to "AND's" to have it all right now.

Dennis' Notes—Being Joyful Now

Awareness: What am I waiting for to happen in my life in order for me to become happy and joyful? Where are my "OR's" & "IF/THEN's"?

Response: How can I be happy today, right now? What will I change to an AND? What reminders can I put in my life to see the joy now, in this present time?

Compassion: Look at how I can change my mood & attitude so quickly. Great job!

Download Dennis' notes at **www.experimenttoday.com/exercises

Laser Focus

ROBERT WAITED FOR this to sink in. "How about we switch around your thinking. From now on, realize that getting in shape and being happier will lead you to profitability at work—not the other way around."

Dennis slowly shook his head in disbelief. "I don't know about that."

"I guarantee you that we can increase what you get done in a day while you actually work less. *And* we'll find time for you to have more energy by working out and eating better."

Dennis wanted to believe Robert, but he really couldn't. His expression must have said as much, because Robert continued, "Okay. Remember what we did last time? Let's just do it again. Try it as an experiment. Can you get on board for that?"

Dennis felt himself relax. "Yeah," he said. "I can do that."

"Great. Let me ask you some questions. How many hours a day do you normally work?"

"On average, ten. Plus I put in a half day most Saturdays. Helps me catch up on administration."

"Do you feel you get what you want done each day?"

Dennis shook his head. "Honestly no. Sometimes I work myself to the bone all day long. Then on the way home I remember I didn't even get done what I wanted to do that day."

"Well, never fear. You're like most people out there. You know how most of what we've talked about so far is 'simple yet complex'?"

"Oh yeah."

"Well this one is simple yet *simple*. On the way into work, think of the three most important things you have to do that day. As soon as you get in, write them down. Then do them."

Dennis spread his hands wide in question. "What's the catch?"

Robert said, "Okay, you're right, there *is* a catch. Do them before anything else. Before talking to anyone, before calling anyone. And most importantly, before opening your e-mail."

"Huh?" Dennis said as he considered Robert's advice. "Before e-mail?"

"Yes. Before anything. Before checking your fantasy football scores, before seeing what your stocks are doing, whatever. Coffee and the bathroom. That's all you're allowed."

"Ha! I guess I'm lucky I get those two."

Robert smiled. "I've had clients try without those two important components and... Well, let's just say that particular experiment had to be adjusted."

"What three things should I choose?"

"Whatever moves your business forward the most. Pick strategic actions. Calls to potential strategic partnerships. Research on future hires in key positions. Touch base with your largest client just because. Cold call a huge prospect yourself. Do all the things that are easy to put off but are really the drivers of your business."

> **Prioritization is the key to consistent, lasting success. When we work on the most important, most strategic items first, they always get done and we leap ahead in our life.**

"Wow. I can see how that would be powerful."

"And don't be afraid to make one of those to-do's something of a personal nature. We often get so busy that we can forget to take care of ourselves."

"I know what you mean."

"Then do the thing you're dreading most first, so it's over with. Getting anything you don't enjoy doing off your list is always a good thing. The result is that you start your day with a win."

"Got it. I can do that."

Dennis' Notes—Laser Focus

Awareness: What are the three most important things I can do today that will move me forward?

Response: I'm writing them down and doing them FIRST THING every day!

Compassion: Look at how I am making progress! Each day I know I'm getting the important things done.

Download Dennis' notes at **www.experimenttoday.com/exercises

Bad Habits to Good Habits

ROBERT NODDED. "GOOD. Now if we're good with that for now, let's move on. You mentioned you were drinking too much."

"Yeah," Dennis said, feeling a pang of guilt. "I always tell myself: *just a few drinks*. But then it always turns into a few more and, well..."

"And how does that work out for you? What's the result?"

"Pretty obvious, I guess. When I get up the next morning, I'm groggy. Sometimes I've got a headache." Dennis reflected for a second. "My energy's low during the day and it affects my mood."

"Do you drink at home or out socially?"

He thought about this for a moment. "Both. Though recently I've been drinking more and more at home."

Robert nodded, unfazed, and said briskly, "Okay. Three things to do. First, find something to do at home besides drink. Something supportive to divert that 'drinking' energy to. Do you read much?"

"Yeah. I love to read. But, well," he looked into his lap as an image of his books came into his mind. "I guess I've got a pile of books that I want to read. But I haven't looked at them recently."

"That's about to change. You can experiment with always having a book around and every time you think about having a drink, tell yourself you'll at least pick up the book for a few minutes. If you still want a drink after reading for ten minutes, go ahead—in moderation. But I'll bet that once you start reading you'll rather keep going with that instead of drinking."

Dennis shrugged, partly convinced. "I can see how that might work."

"Second, at home, make getting a drink a chore. Put your booze somewhere hard to get to. Wrap it up in something or put it on a shelf that you need to climb a ladder to get to. Every time you want a drink, make yourself go through a process to get it. Make yourself work for it."

Dennis grinned. "You know, I can see how that would make it more of a conscious decision to get a drink."

"Super. Lastly, whether you're at home or out, instead of limiting yourself to a 'few' drinks, tell yourself 'two' drinks. Two is a finite number your brain can't stretch into 'many.' The fact is, when we're specific, we stop. When we're vague, we give ourselves too much leeway and interpret our circumstances to suit what we want at the time."

> **The three strategies to *stop* doing something are to: find a more uplifting activity to refocus energy on; make it as difficult as possible to engage in the bad habit; and lastly set very specific limits around what you are committing to control.**

"Done," Dennis said, slightly surprised. "At least it *sounds* easy."

"It *is* easy. Often the best solutions are simple." He smiled. "Now, how about working out? What have you done before? What do you like and not like to do? Any sports?"

"Well, I've taken aerobics classes because they worked for both strength and cardio. But I really didn't like them. I *do* love tennis, but I haven't played it in over a year."

"Then I would consider tennis over aerobics," Robert said with a chuckle.

"Ha, ha," Dennis said. "But you know at this point I wouldn't know where to start."

"Well let's think about that, then. What's the first step you'd have to take?"

Dennis smiled. "Find my racket."

"Okay, then. Why not take one small step every day. Day one: find a racket. Day two: buy a new one if you need to. Day three: find courts around your area. Day four: find someone to play with. And so on."

Dennis sighed. "You make it all seem so doable." He shook his head in bewilderment. "Why do I make things so hard on myself when they can be so easy?"

Robert gave him a friendly smile as he said gently, "Dennis, remember our compassion! Getting down on yourself isn't going to help; it's just going to drain your energy. Patting yourself on the back will lift you up and give you more energy. That's been scientifically proven."

"There's research on that?"

"There sure is. A study by the Mayo Clinic showed that optimists live nineteen percent longer. Other studies have found that joyful people are more productive and have a higher income."

"Really?"

"You bet. In one study, researchers gave 255 subjects a test that measured hostility. In twenty-five years, heart disease appeared in the angriest people about five times as often as in the least angry ones."

"Wow. Thinking about it, I've always thought it was simply *nice* to be happy. I didn't realize it could help me make money and live longer!"

> **Taking an optimistic view—which *can* be learned—leads to better decision making, job performance and achievement, as well as to more overall energy.**

Robert nodded in agreement. "It's great, isn't it? Now, that's a lot I've given you today. Are you willing to try all that for a week?"

"You bet."

"Wonderful." Robert went to stand up but then paused. "You know, you're really great to work with Dennis. You really go for it."

"Really? I don't always feel like that. I have so many issues—which you're helping me with, of course."

"It's not the number of issues one has or doesn't have. It's how you approach them. In your case, you're willing to change and experiment. And you know, the fact is that your issues aren't really that different from anyone else's. We're all just good at hiding them from view."

"Well, I really want to change. I'm tired of the way I've been living life. I know the more I put into this the faster I'll get where I want to go." A thought occurred to him then, and he said, "Hey, one question for you. Do you have a coach?"

Robert nodded. "You bet I do. Even though I deal with other people's issues every day, I need the same guidance from someone on the outside looking in at *me*. It's impossible to look at my own life from 30,000 feet when I'm in it every day."

Dennis smiled as they stood up together. "That makes me feel better."

"I've never met anyone who couldn't benefit from a coach."

Dennis' Notes—Bad Habits to Good Habits

Awareness: What am I doing now that I can do less of, or eliminate, to improve my life?

Examples: Smoking, drinking, watching trashy TV

What can I replace these things with?

Response: How am I going to rearrange my life so I start doing more of the good and less of the negative by finding replacements and making it more difficult to do the unhealthy things… and easier to do the healthy things?

Compassion: Look at the changes I am making in my life that are truly making a difference. Bravo!

Download Dennis' notes at **www.experimenttoday.com/exercises

Changes in Action

ON THE WAY home Dennis picked up some fruit juice and made a commitment to himself that he wouldn't buy beer in the grocery store. Nor would he grab a beer after work. He'd still have a beer or two when he was out with buddies—but *only* two, at most. That would be it. And he wouldn't drink it at home.

When he arrived home he made some changes. He put his alcohol in the garage, which was far enough away to deter him. He went through his bookshelf, took out three books he hadn't read, and put them on his coffee table. He was feeling so good that he went for a walk that turned into a light jog halfway through. That night he slept better than he had in months and woke up feeling refreshed.

When Dennis got to work that next day, he went to his desk, took out a piece of paper and wrote down:

1. Call Marie to say we can't finish the prototype in the original timeframe

This was a call that he had been putting off because he was sure Marie would be angry with him. He never liked delivering bad news.

Then he wrote down the second item:

2. Cindy—Employee Review

Cindy was supposed to have gotten her review months ago. He kept putting it off because he was so busy, and he could tell that she was getting frustrated. She moved mountains for him on a daily basis and he knew she needed the recognition for it; she looked forward to the meeting every year.

3. Buy a Tennis Racket

He picked up the phone and dialed Marie. She picked up immediately.

"Hi Marie. It's Dennis."

"Hi Dennis. I'm glad to hear from you. You were on my list to call today anyway."

"I wanted to catch you up on that prototype. Our guys have been working hard on it, and we've even put an extra guy on, at no cost to you. A senior guy."

"That sounds great, Dennis. But you must be calling for a reason."

He grimaced but pressed on. "That's right, Marie. I wanted to let you know it's going to be delayed another two weeks. I know that's not what you want to hear, but you have my word it's not for lack of effort."

There was a brief pause on the other end of the line, then Marie said, "That's okay, Dennis. I appreciate you being proactive and letting me know now, rather than after the deadline. You'll keep me in the loop if the target changes again?"

"Of course. Thanks for understanding. We want to get it right."

When the call was over he put down the phone with a sigh of relief. She was okay with it being late because he had called proactively—and he called her today instead of the other way around. The call had not been a nightmare; in fact it was pretty smooth. He began to wonder what would have happened if he hadn't made the call today, then kicked that thought out of his mind. *No use going down that path,* he thought. *This is the new way forward!*

Cindy's review went stellar and only took fifteen minutes. She left beaming, and he was feeling good too. A huge smile and "Thanks, boss!" as she left capped the amazing meeting. Again he started to wonder why he had taken so long to get to it. And again he remembered to have compassion for himself. He smiled at the thought. He really *was* retraining that voice inside his head!

Ten minutes on Amazon.com and he had a tennis racket coming to his house in two days.

Thirty minutes into his day and he had already gotten a ton accomplished. It felt good.

Session 3

Experiments Work

A WEEK LATER, DENNIS came into Robert's office wearing a huge grin, hardly able to curb his enthusiasm. He opened with, "I've been waiting to tell you what's been happening."

Robert rubbed his hands together. "Great! I'm excited to hear."

"The three things a day is a great system! I'm getting more done than I ever thought possible—and first thing in the morning! It's like the rest of the day is just icing on the cake. Makes me feel so good, so productive."

Robert returned Dennis' smile. "That's super. Sounds like you're no longer a victim of your tasks, and that you've moved on to be an owner of them. And you know what? It becomes easier and easier as you keep at it."

Dennis nodded and said, "And I've been drinking less, too. *Much* less. And at home—not at all. I don't even miss it. *And* I've finished a book in the short time since we last met."

He hesitated before adding, "But I have to admit I went to a friend's party. A buddy drove, and I drank way more than two drinks. I didn't even set the goal of only two drinks. I knew we were having a night of it."

Robert shrugged and said gently, "That's alright, Dennis. Really. This whole process is about moderation. And it's excellent that you were very responsible and mindful about your drinking. You had a driver, you knew you were planning to, as you say, 'make a night of it,' and so you didn't break any agreements that you made with yourself." He smiled. "We're all allowed to let loose once in a while. If you want my take on it, what you did was fine. Now just jump right back up on the wagon. Make sure nights out, particularly like that one, don't become a frequent habit, and maybe work out a little extra the next day. It's a special occasion type of thing. That's another level of compassion for yourself. Being okay with your choices and being human."

Dennis felt relieved; part of him had been concerned that Robert would admonish him for cutting loose at the party. "Great, Robert. That helps a lot. Thanks." He smiled again and said, "Now for some more good news: I played tennis with a buddy yesterday. We had so much fun, but man am I sore!"

Robert laughed. "I'm not surprised! That, of course, will get easier with time too. I'm sure you see now: these changes don't have to be that difficult." He leaned forward and looked Dennis in the eye. "So, this past week was an experiment. Are you now ready to take things out of the experimental stage and make them *habits?*"

There was no doubt in Dennis' mind. "Yes, definitely!" he said.

Then without warning his mood abruptly changed and he let out a long sigh.

Laura

ROBERT ASKED, "What is it?"

Dennis shook his head. "You know, I'm *so* happy with this stuff. I don't want it to stop. But I just thought of the disaster with my wife, Laura, and my kids, Sadie and Jacob... That one seems unsolvable. And it's hard to imagine being really happy until I *do* solve it."

Robert sat back in his chair and said simply, "Tell me more."

"Laura hates me. Really hates me. I still love her, but every time I do something for her she gets angry at me. And..."

"Hold on a second Dennis," Robert interjected. "Slow down. What exactly do you mean by saying that every time you do something for her she gets angry?"

"Well, for example, just before she took the kids and moved out, I bought her an expensive necklace. I thought it would make her happy. But when I gave it to her she just looked at me and started to cry!"

"Why do you think she did that?"

"I have no idea!"

"Then guess. Why do you think? What could have been going through her head when she started crying?"

Dennis took a deep breath and remained silent. The more he sat there, the clearer the answer became. He said, "She keeps telling me she wants us to be closer." Dennis paused, thinking. "She wants me to spend more time at home. With the family." Again a pause. "I wasn't doing that so I bought her the necklace instead." He shrugged, feeling embarrassed. It was so obvious when he thought about it. "She was angry at me for trying to buy her off instead of spending time with her. I'm such an idiot. I deserve this. I deserve to be alone."

Robert jumped in. "Dennis, you're doing great here. You've got to think these things through, and you're doing that. But remember the 'C' in 'ARC'—compassion. We all have great power. That power comes from us *choosing* how to respond to different things. And you just took the correct first step by taking ownership for your actions in that situation with your wife. Now, instead of judging yourself, can you perhaps consider *honoring* yourself for opening up to someone—me—and putting yourself in a place to learn and grow as a human?"

It was hard to shake off his negative feelings, but Dennis managed to muster up: "I guess so."

"See, Dennis, we're all doing the best we can at any point in time. We have limited information, and a lot is happening, so we do the best we can. Getting angry at yourself for the choices you made at any given time is fruitless. The same goes for getting upset with anyone else for *their* choices. It's really just wasted energy. And look at yourself honestly, Dennis. You've done so much for the world. Look at all you've created."

> **Everyone is always making the best decisions they can all the time. Judging other people for the choices they've made, and ourselves for the ones we've made, is pointless and a waste of energy. Everyone is better served looking forward, not backward.**

Relationships & Love

DENNIS HAD KEPT HIS head bowed while Robert was talking. Now he looked up.

Robert continued, "Would it be safe to say that you love your wife and kids?"

"Absolutely."

"How do you think you show love, Dennis?"

This gave Dennis pause. "I don't know. I hadn't really thought about it."

"Now's a good time to look at that. When you care for someone, how do you show it? How did you show it to your wife in that last example?"

"I bought something for her."

"A lot of business people show their love by trying to help the people they love in a particular way. They buy them things. They solve their problems. They 'fix' their lives. Though that's just one aspect of the relationship. Do you think you might do that with your kids?"

"Hmmm. I guess I do. I want the best for them. So I give them advice. I tell them how they can do better." He felt slightly defensive as he said, "I just want the very best for them."

> **Deep relationships are never formed through "fixing" problems and giving advice. Closeness, connection and intimacy come through authentic communication and vulnerability with others. And through giving others attention in the way *they* want to receive it.**

"Yes I can really see how you love them. And I'm sure they get great advantages from you in that way. But let me ask you this: how do you think *they* want to receive love?"

The question caught Dennis off guard, and he had no answer for it. "Wow," he said. "I definitely never thought of that."

"When you were a kid, did you like getting advice from your dad?"

"Uh—not really." He chuckled. "Actually it pissed me off. He was always telling me how to do things. Never said he was proud of me or anything."

"Now... Could that be your son Jacob talking?"

Dennis was silent.

Robert continued, "How did you want your dad to love you when you were young?"

"I guess... I guess I just wanted him to accept me. To tell me he was proud of me. To hang out with me and just spend time with me."

"Do you do that with your kids now?"

Dennis' shoulders dropped. He gave a dejected, "No. Just like my dad did to me. Here I am doing the same thing that was so hurtful to me." He felt a tear run down his cheek but he was too sad to be embarrassed by it.

Robert interrupted his mood. "Dennis, look up at me. This is all okay. It's great, really, because you're showing me—and yourself—how you really feel. And as of right now you can change how you approach this. Think about it—for generations your family has most likely been behaving the same way. Your parents, theirs before that and so on. But, really, it's no one's fault. No one came along and said, 'Here, let me show you how to do this.' They didn't have anyone to study this and teach it to them. But now it's your turn. *You* can bring these new tools and skills—the same ones we've been talking about these past few weeks—into your family. You can break this intergenerational pattern. And once you change it, for generations to come your family will be happier and closer. Think of yourself as a change agent for your family—past, present and future."

Many habits and behaviors, good and bad, get passed down to us through our families. Just like any other habits, though, they are changeable. Victims choose to complain about the hand they were dealt. Owners take control and change what they want to change.

The prospect gave a new sparkle to Dennis's eyes. Then he asked, "But what about my wife? How would I know how she wants to receive love?"

"Well, asking her is a great start. Though I think you already know, or at least have a good idea."

"Well... She wants to spend time with me. To become close. To talk, like we used to."

"Yes. And do you enjoy doing that with her? Spending time with her?"

"I do. A lot, actually. It just seems there's never enough time."

"Think back to what we've talked about already. With exercise, for example. Is it really true there's not enough time?"

Dennis didn't really need to think about this. He said firmly, "No, it's not. That's just me playing the victim, isn't it? Just like with tennis and exercise. I've learned it's up to me to make it happen."

"That's right."

"But, you know, she's got blame here too! She—"

"Stop right there." Robert up raised his hand. "This isn't about assigning blame. If you want to go down that road, do it with someone else. I teach people how to solve issues in their lives, not figure out who's more to blame."

Dennis smiled. "Got me, Yoda."

Robert laughed. "That's okay. There's always a lot of energy around things like this. Keep talking from where you left off."

"Okay... She's pretty angry with me right now. I need to figure out how to make things work better."

Dennis' Notes—Relationships

Awareness: Regarding an important relationship in my life, how am I showing up? And is that what the person wants from me?

Response: How will I authentically communicate my expectations? How can I learn the others' expectations?
I will match my actions to what the other person likes, as long as I'm still being genuine and it's within my healthy boundaries.

Compassion: I'm compassionate and fully accepting of both myself and the other person in the relationship.

Download Dennis' notes at **www.experimenttoday.com/exercises

Laura, Part 2

ROBERT NODDED AND said, "You have to start somewhere, and it may take some time, so don't try to force it. But
then again, sometimes profound change happens like this—
" and he snapped his fingers.

"Can it really be that easy?" Dennis asked.

"It certainly can. But it's important that you keep in mind
you can only control yourself—your actions, what you say
and do. She may or may not respond in the way you hope she
does. And whatever happens, you have to respect her decisions."

"Are you talking about not being tied to the outcome?"

"Yes, exactly. Because if you say, for example, that you'll
only be happy if she comes back to you, then your success
and happiness is dependent on what she does or doesn't do.
But what you're trying to achieve may or may not happen
quickly—or even at all. Although in my experience, when you
come to the table with compassion, positive energy and the

intention to understand and move forward together, you're normally met with a positive response."

> **When we link our happiness to whether something happens or doesn't happen, we give up our freedom. Instead, we can focus on showing up in the absolute best way we can, and prize ourselves for that.**

Just then Dennis's phone rang, startling him; Robert seemed unfazed. Dennis said apologetically, "I had it on 'do-not-disturb.' It must be an important call if it actually rang. Do you mind if I take it?"

"Go ahead," said Robert.

Dennis glanced at the screen and saw it was his wife. He glanced at Robert. "It's her," he said with a slight smile as he stood up. "Time to try a new approach."

"Hi, Laura."

A loud, angry voice came through on the other end.

"Dennis, I've had enough! I need a break. Sadie got into trouble at school again! You've got to step up and—"

Dennis interrupted gently, "Yes, Laura. Yes. I understand. You know what? I know this has been tough on you, too." Laura remained silent on the other end; he imagined she was too surprised to speak. An idea occurred to him, and he said, "Can I suggest something for this weekend?"

Laura found her voice. "Don't try to back out of taking the kids!"

Dennis kept his voice calm as he said, "Just hear me out. How about this? I'd like to spend Saturday with Sadie and Sunday with Jacob. I think it's time for me to spend one-on-one time with each of our kids. Then you can do the same with the other kid, okay?" Before she could reply he added, "And I'll take them both on Friday to give you a day off. You deserve it, I know." She remained silent, so he took a chance and said, "And one day next week, if it's okay with you, I'd like your mom to watch the kids. I'll come over to the house, or you come over to ours, and I'll cook you dinner. I... we can try having a nice night together. Okay?"

Laura said hesitantly, "Are... are you feeling okay, Dennis?"

Dennis smiled. "Yes, Laura, I'm fine. Would you mind if I talked to Sadie?" As Laura went to get her he started pacing, then paused, covered the mouthpiece of the phone and said to Robert, "My daughter just got in trouble again at school, I bet for hitting other kids. And she's only eight years old."

At that moment Sadie came on the line. Dennis said, "Hi Sadie. Tough day, honey?"

A small, hesitant voice said, "Yes."

"Honey, I'm sure things must be tough right now, and—no, I'm not going to yell at you. In fact, what I want to say is that I love you and I'm proud of you. And there may be a better way to go about things than hitting other kids."

"But, daddy, they were—"

"That's okay, honey. I really can't tell because I wasn't there, but we can talk about it all this weekend. I'm working that out with your mom right now. Would you mind putting her back on?" He couldn't help but smile as she, too, said,

"Daddy, are you feeling okay?"

"I'm fine, Sadie, really. Can you get mom?"

Dennis covered the mouthpiece again and said to Robert, "She was bracing for me to yell at her, which is—was—my normal behavior. Then she asked if I was okay!" He wore a big smile.

"Hi Laura. Yes, again, I'm okay. I'm just trying a, well, a new approach to things."

She said, "Well, I like it."

"Thanks. So I'll see you Friday? Great. Love you. Bye."

She gave him a hesitant, "Love you, too," as she said goodbye.

Authenticity and Vulnerability

DENNIS SIGHED AS HE sat back down. "I feel like I just defused a bomb. Before, that conversation would have sent me into a tailspin. It would have drained my energy and been on my mind for hours. Now I feel good. Energized, even!"

Robert said, "When we show up bringing positivity into a previously dark situation, we're rewarded. Rewarded with energy for ourselves, and from other people. We often get loyalty, respect and admiration."

> **When we bring love and compassion forward, it is most often met with the same. It's up to each of us to take the lead and change the whole tone of the conversation.**

Robert leaned forward and added, "We sometimes think that accepting blame and showing vulnerability can be a sign of weakness. Really, though, it's a sign of strength. Think about it from this perspective: when you see someone denying something that you know they did, what do you think of them?"

"Not much," Dennis replied.

"How about when you see someone owning up to something?"

"I respect them."

"Me too. Sometimes it's hard to remember, but leaders who accept full responsibility, leaders who show that they *aren't* perfect are the ones people want to follow."

Dennis nodded thoughtfully. "I'm beginning to see that."

"Good. Then let's talk about all this when it comes to your staff."

"How do you mean?"

"Tell me about your staff meetings. Do you ever get everyone in the company all together?"

"Yeah, once a quarter. Everyone gets together for an all-hands meeting."

"And how do they go?"

"Well, I used to be so inspired to get up there and talk about how great we were doing. It gave me a real rush, and I felt really connected to the company. But over the past few years, as business has become tougher, our quarterly all-staff meetings have gone downhill. Now I have to force *myself* to be upbeat." He gave Robert a sheepish look. "And, honestly, I don't think it comes off very well."

Robert said, "Let me guess. You feel like a fraud because you're not being totally truthful, and you're afraid people can sense that?"

Dennis was surprised at how spot on that guess was. He said, "Wow. Exactly. Yes."

"Well, you're probably right. People have good instincts. Call it intuition, if you like. And everyone can smell B.S. a mile away. They might not always know exactly what's going on, but they can tell when something's wrong, when things don't exactly fit together. So let me ask you this: why are you holding back? Why aren't you getting up there and saying what's really on your mind?"

"I... I guess..." Dennis faltered, trying to find the right words. "I feel like they expect me to be perfect, so I need to give the impression that I am. I guess... Well, to be honest, it's hard to get up there and admit that things aren't great. I'm the boss, the owner after all."

"So they expect you to be perfect?"

Dennis thought for a minute. "Well, no. I guess I expect myself to be perfect—or to at least show that things are perfect."

"Do you expect that of others?"

The words came easily: "No. Of course not."

"Try telling the truth. The real truth. Because if you stand up there and deliver what people know isn't the truth, you actually push them away. They lose trust in you."

"So what do I do?" Dennis felt genuinely perplexed. "Dump all my problems on the staff?"

"There's a way to be authentic about both the positive *and* negatives while bringing your team closer together. Do they know it's a tough time in the industry?"

"Yeah. In fact, they know a lot of our competitors have laid people off."

"And have you had to do the same?"

"No. We're proud of the fact that we haven't had to do that."

"That's impressive. That's something you could rally around. It's tough in the industry, but your goal as a company is to weather the storm with your staff intact. You can say to them, 'Let's double our efforts, increase our focus, do what we can to keep everyone employed—and make a gain in the market while others are losing.'"

"It sounds pretty good when *you* say it."

Robert laughed. "And when you say it, it will sound even better."

"I guess I can see what you're getting at. This can work. It doesn't have to be a death march. It can be us pulling together. Getting stronger."

Intimacy and trust are created through vulnerability. The way we connect with others is by relating to them, not by pretending everything's perfect.

"Exactly." Robert leaned back and arched his brows. "Ready for one more experiment?"

Reconnect with Your Joy

DENNIS FELT EXCITEMENT stirring within him. He said with conviction, "Yes, I am. Give me more! I'm ready."

"Great. The reason we need to teach ourselves new habits is because oftentimes our brains are taught to pick out problems. As a business executive, you often have to look at problems and isolate what's wrong in order to fix them. These could be sales or cash flow problems, or whatever. And, certainly, your people always come to you with problems for you to help fix."

Dennis thought about this. "Yeah, that's true. Whenever someone comes to me it's with a problem. Whenever I review something I'm looking to see what's wrong with it."

Robert nodded. "This is the norm nowadays. But one of the side effects of doing things this way is that it gets us stuck in a pattern of focusing on the negative. So we need to retrain our brains. We want to move from focusing on negatives to being able to easily and quickly notice the positives."

"I think I know what you mean," Dennis said. "My work life is normally about finding and fixing problems. Now that I think about it, even my home life seems that way. It's depressing!"

"It can certainly feel that way. But the good news is that it doesn't *have* to be that way. Here's how to create habits of positivity and reconnect with that feeling of joy inside you. Each evening I'd like you to spend a few minutes reviewing how your day went. Have a journal at hand and list in it three things: what you're grateful for, what you've done well that day, and what's gone your way. Got that?"

Dennis nodded in agreement. "Yep. Each night, take out a journal, and write down what I'm thankful for, what I've done well, and when I've gotten lucky?"

"That's right. We write down what we're thankful for in order to train ourselves to be joyful in our everyday lives. This could be for something as simple as a hot shower or a fast car we enjoy driving, or it could be something deeper, such as a loving relative. What we're doing is training ourselves to *enjoy* our lives more by being more conscious of all the little things we take for granted."

"I get it. I know that's something I could be better at, that's for sure."

"Most of us can. Now in step two we write down what we've done well in order to show ourselves that we have great capabilities, and also to build more confidence in our inherent abilities. This lets us trust ourselves more and reduces stress. Remember, stress often comes from trying to control situations that we can't control."

Dennis thought about this then said, "That's true. When I think about what I've accomplished, some of what I seem to stress about seems pretty insignificant."

"Well, we forget how adept we really are at so many things. So it helps to remind ourselves daily."

> **When we remember how capable we are, we don't have to worry about every little possibility. We know that we can handle whatever comes up. We have fantastic capacities; keeping that in mind gives us the confidence and the energy to naturally take on the day's challenges.**

Robert gave Dennis that familiar warm smile and said, "Now last but not least, write down where the universe has smiled upon us, as I like to say, to remind ourselves that the world is a good, giving, positive place. This opens us up to more good fortune—even to miracles, if you can believe it.

Again, this reduces stress as we remember how many good things happen to us every day."

"I'm beginning to get it."

"That's great, Dennis. Now when you're journaling at night and find there's an area you want to focus on the next day—for example, someone at work did a good job and you want to acknowledge them, or you want to treat yourself to a massage—make a note of that in another area for the next day. Then, in the morning, review everything you wrote in that spot the night before. You'll find that it gives you a lift to start your day. It also reminds you to prioritize what came to you when you were reflecting."

Dennis said, "Sounds easy. I'll give it a try."

Robert shook his head and said firmly, "Do or not do. There is no try."

Dennis wrinkled his brow and said, "Did you just quote Yoda to me?"

Robert grinned. "Ahhh, busted!"

This made them both laugh.

"Question for you, Robert," Dennis said. "Am I a typical client? Does it always happen this way?"

"Well, not really, no. Everyone is different, of course. Some people take more time to see that their old patterns are keeping them in the same place. Occasionally I run across someone who won't ever change their behavior, someone who isn't open to suggestions."

"What do you do then?"

Robert shrugged. "I simply don't work with them. That may sound harsh, but I've found that the only thing that stops people is not being open to experimenting. That's why the only requirement I have is that you do the work. If you do the work, changes will happen."

"I hear that. I'm living it. I just wish I was a better client. I seem to have so many issues."

"Nonsense! In fact, you're really a *great* client. People come to me with all sorts of different things they want to change in their lives. It's not about quantity. It's about mindset and the intention to change. And what I've seen in you, Dennis, is that you go for it! You've been doing so since that very first intention you stated when we started working together."

> It's never about where we are at now, it's about the *ferocity* with which we focus our attention on improving those areas. It's the courage that we show when experimenting with new ways of living life, because doing so leaves us vulnerable.

Dennis suddenly felt an overwhelming sense of gratitude. "I have to tell you, Robert, that my life has changed dramatically in an incredibly short time. Thank you. Truly. It's like you're helping me put my life back together—the right way. I had almost given up hope. I thought I would have to live the same way for the rest of my life. What good is everything I've accomplished if I'm not happy?"

Robert smiled, and Dennis could feel the warmth coming from him. "Thank *you*, Dennis. And I agree.

"Because what is success without happiness?"

Dennis' Notes—Reconnect with Joy

I will print this and fill it out in the evening. I'll write what I want to focus on the next day. Then I'll review it in the morning.

My Gratitude—What I'm thankful for. This helps my mind start recognizing all the good things in my life.
I'll note down anything/everything.
-Wow the hot shower felt good this morning
-What a super hug from my kid
-A sunny day on the way to work
-My comfy chair in the office

My Impact—What I did right today. I do so many good things in a day; time to own that.
-I remembered to kiss my spouse on the way out and make them feel good
-Had a conversation with an employee that I was putting off, and turned out it really energized them

My Prosperity—What went my way today? I'll list all the chance happenings that favored me. Then I'll remember that I'm lucky and fortunate.

-I got that VIP parking space

-The callback from the huge prospect I thought I lost a few months ago

My Gratitude	My Impact	My Prosperity

Tomorrow I will remember to: _____

Epilogue

TWO YEARS LATER, DENNIS was sitting on the train on his way to work. He had just gotten off the phone with Leslie, his banker. A year and a half before this, Bob had taken over as VP of Sales and the company had started to grow again. Now talking with Leslie was an absolute pleasure. In fact, Dennis and Leslie had just planned a trip together with their spouses to go wine tasting the following weekend. Dennis and Laura were back together, and things were going great. Their relationship was better than it had ever been before.

Dennis watched as a man got on the train, his arms wrapped around a pile of papers, his laptop case falling off his shoulder. He looked as if he could drop it all at any second.

The man plopped down next to Dennis with a sigh. A few stray papers fell to the floor and his mobile phone began ringing. Dennis picked up the man's papers and watched him fish around in his pocket to find his phone. He said, "Hello?" into the phone. Even over the rumble of the train, Dennis could hear someone yelling at the man from the other end of the line. The man shouted back, "I'm on the train! I can't deal with this right now!" and hung up angrily. He looked down to pick up the papers he dropped, and when he didn't immediately see them a look of panic came into his eyes.

Dennis handed him the papers. He got the sense this guy wasn't used to getting help from others.

He said, "Thanks. Ugh. I'm sorry for shouting just then. My car broke down. My life is really hectic right now. I grabbed everything and ran to catch the train."

Dennis said, "That's how I started to ride the train too." He thought back to that day, just over two years ago, when his own car had broken down. That seemed so far away. "Now I actually prefer the train to my car. I use the ride to collect my thoughts as I head into the office. And I make sure I make the four-thirty train back so I'm not in the office all day."

The man looked incredulous. "Four-thirty? I haven't left the office earlier than eight o'clock at night any day this month. The only reason I'm on the train this early is I gotta go home to catch the repair man. You must have it easier than I do. My company's having problems. The economy's down and my wife hates me." He shook his head and let out a low whistle. "Man, it sounds like you've got it made. You're a lucky man."

Dennis said gently, "I wasn't so different from you not long ago. Come to think of it, I was right where you're at now."

"Yeah? What changed? I need something." He laughed without humor. "A miracle."

"That's what I thought too. My miracle came in the form of a coach. I met him right here on this train, two years ago, in fact."

"A coach? He gives you advice?"

Dennis thought about that then said, "Sometimes, though that isn't what it's about. He slows me down and helps me walk through things. We still meet whenever I need him."

"I'm not sure if I could ever go to a coach."

"Why not?"

"Well, he wouldn't know my industry. And I'm just too busy."

Dennis laughed, but it was at the thought of his old self rather than the man next to him. "Funny, that's exactly what I said."

"How'd you find time?"

"I made time. I was tired of living like you are now."

This apparently made the man think, for he looked down at the floor for a moment before responding, "Yeah, well, I'm not sure I could commit to a coach."

Dennis said, "Well, you don't have to commit. Just try it. **Think of it as an experiment...**"

What's Your Experiment?

Excited? Great! Go to http://tiny.cc/my-xpmt to take the next step;

- Declare *your* Experiment!
- Get support and encouragement direct from me, R. Michael Anderson
- Download printable copies of the exercises in this book

Remember, *the only way you fail in an experiment is by not trying it.*

***One more thing...**please REVIEW ME!** Take a minute, rate the book and give it an HONEST review, even just a few lines, on Amazon: http://tiny.cc/review-xpmt

This lets prospective future readers know about your experience and gives me feedback for upcoming books.

Many Thanks!

-R. Michael Anderson

Continue with *The Experiment*

Interesting in bringing Experiments into your work, group or personal life?

The author, R. Michael Anderson, M.B.A, M.A., and his company **Executive Joy!**, provide the following services:

- Speaking
- Corporate Training
- Facilitation
- Retreats
- Coaching

Contact us at info@executivejoy.com or visit www.executivejoy.com to learn more. Mention you are a reader of *The Experiment* when contacting us for special pricing and other extras.

About the Author

R. (ROBERT) MICHAEL ANDERSON, M.B.A., M.A., is an international speaker, radio-show host and author who specializes in leading competitive, driven people through the same transformation that he's been through, bringing joy and happiness into their lives.

Even though he had played professional basketball (yes, he's really six-foot nine!), founded three international software companies, and partied at the Playboy mansion, he simply wasn't happy. Drugs, alcohol, a divorce and a nasty lawsuit brought him to a low point.

A quest for change included earning a Master's Degree in Spiritual Psychology from the prestigious University of Santa Monica.